W9-CFF-550

1

Meditations for the New Mother

"He shall gather the lambs with his arm, and carry them in his bosom, and shall gently lead those that are with young." ISAIAH 40:11b

Meditations for the New Mother

By

HELEN GOOD BRENNEMAN

Drawings By

ESTHER ROSE GRABER

A devotional book for
the new mother during the first
month following the birth
of her baby

HERALD PRESS
SCOTTDALE, PENNSYLVANIA

To my own dear mother
who first revealed to me
the beauty of motherhood

Preface

Today you are a *mother*. Beside you lies a little soul, wrapped in the swaddling clothes of innocency, purity, love, and trust. Where he has come from, you do not really know; how you deserve him, you will never understand; what lies in store for him, only the future will reveal. In him is life which will survive the ages, and even now he is a part of things eternal, for Jesus said, "Of such is the kingdom of heaven."

All in all, you have had a momentous experience, and joy has been written into every chapter of it. There was personal joy, an unequaled thrill over the baby's first cry. There was family joy, for the coming of the new member draws parents closer together than ever before. There was spiritual joy, for you have co-operated with God your Maker in the wonderful creation of a new life.

Great moments in one's life are never without their special problems, though, and certainly new motherhood has its full share. You may have thought that you had fully prepared for the coming of the little basket-dweller, but there are many details which now require your constant attention. The *human* infant is the most helpless of all God's babies, and all the answers are not to be found in the baby book!

Doctors will tell you that while your strength is coming back, physical and glandular changes are taking place in your body which can affect your emotional life. And since one's spiritual life is so closely associated with one's physical and emotional well-being, you no doubt feel the need of the loving presence of God in a very special way at this time.

It is as a result of my own experience of new motherhood, with its accompanying joys and problems, that I have prepared this little book of *Meditations for the New Mother,* a collection of Scriptures, poetry, and devotional thoughts especially meaningful after the birth of a baby. My prayer is that the rich passages of the Word of God will not only inspire you during that first important month of your baby's life, but will continue to guide you in your lifelong task of motherhood.

Perhaps I should make an apology to mothers of baby girls. In o r d e r to avoid calling the baby "it," I had to use the word "he" throughout the book. However, I hope you will not have too much trouble substituting the words "she," "her," and "hers."

I wish to thank especially Mary Royer, Ph.D., Goshen College, Goshen, Indiana, and my husband, Virgil Brenneman, as well as many other friends for their kind help and encouragement in the completion of this book.

Iowa City, Iowa   HELEN GOOD BRENNEMAN

Contents

III. "Therefore . . . I have lent him to the Lord"

OUR RESPONSIBILITY TO THE CHILD

I. "For this child I prayed . . ."

THANKSGIVING FOR THE CHILD

"For this child I prayed; and the Lord hath given me my petition which I asked of him: therefore also I have lent him to the Lord; as long as he liveth he shall be lent to the Lord."

I SAMUEL 1:27, 28

The Fruit of Your Womb

"Lo, children are an heritage of the Lord:
  And the fruit of the womb is his reward.
As arrows are in the hand of a mighty man;
  So are children of the youth.
Happy is the man that hath his quiver full of them."

PSALM 127:3, 4, 5a

At the dawn of the world, in the morning of time, God looked down upon the beautiful earth which He had made and climaxed His creation by placing a man and a woman in the first home. Now life together for the world's first married couple must have been romantic and very happy, for they loved one another, and their garden-home was exquisitely furnished.

Yet God, in His wisdom, knew that two young people, however much in love, needed something to lift them above themselves and make their affection of a deeper, more lasting nature. Indeed, so great had been His satisfaction in creating this young couple that the Father, wishing to share His creative joy, commanded them to be fruitful, to multiply, and to replenish the earth.

Thus began family life on the earth, and so bearing and bringing up children has continued throughout the ages to be a tender and joyful experience. Thus it was several ages later when David, king and father, wrote of the happiness that comes with children, the heritage of the Lord. Thus it was that Jesus Himself took the babies of His day into His arms to bless them. And thus it is for *you*, today, New Mother, as you join hands with the mothers of the ages, praising the Lord your Maker for the fruit of your womb, your reward and heritage of the Lord, your new baby!

O God, my heavenly Father, I thank Thee with all my heart for the beautiful experience of motherhood and for the baby at my side. Just as Thou hast helped the mothers of all ages, guide me in my new task, bless my precious baby, and bless the baby's father in his love and concern for both of us. Amen.

A MOTHER

God sought to give the sweetest thing
  In His almighty power
To earth; and deeply pondering
  What it should be, one hour
In fondest joy and love of heart
  Outweighing every other,
He moved the gates of heaven apart
  And gave to earth a mother.

AUTHOR UNKNOWN

A babe in a house is a wellspring of pleasure.

M. F. TOPPER

Hannah's Song

"And Hannah prayed, and said,
My heart rejoiceth in the Lord,
Mine horn is exalted in the Lord. . . .
There is none holy as the Lord:
For there is none beside thee:
Neither is there any rock like our God."

Read I Samuel 2:1-10.

Truly the story of Hannah is a woman's story; it is a mother's story. Our hearts beat sympathetically with the heart of this would-be mother who so much desired a child that "she wept, and did not eat." Can you not see her at the temple as "in bitterness of soul" she "prayed unto the Lord, and wept sore"? None of us who have felt that God-given hunger for motherhood and for the warmth of a baby in our arms would censure her for the agreement which she made with God. The Father Himself did not reprove her for it but answered her prayer, accepted her child, and used him mightily in His kingdom. And then, to end the story beautifully, He gave her three more sons and two daughters to bless her life and to make her home complete.

Little Samuel was a *wanted* child and his earliest years were filled with his mother's love. Moreover, Hannah did not forget the Lord when her prayer was answered, as so many do today. When her child was weaned, she took him to the temple, gave him to the Lord, and uttered a prayer that has come down to us through the ages. The prayer expresses joy in her God, victory over her difficulties, stability founded upon the Rock of her salvation, humility, strength, and justice.

Let us today follow Hannah's example as we, too, "praise the Lord for his goodness, and for his wonderful works to the children of men!"

O Lord, my refuge and my fortress, my rock, in whom I trust, I praise Thee for the protection of Thy wings and for the strength of Thy presence. I thank Thee also for laying this little child in my arms to love and to cherish. Help me, his mother, always to dwell under the shadow of the Almighty, in the secret place of the most High. Amen.

HIS CRADLE

It rocked and rocked for joy,
*   This battered world,*
When Mary's little boy
*   Up in it curled,*
*   Despite its chill.*
*   O may He fill*
Today His chosen bed,
*   Through you and me,*
Who love and help to spread
*   Simplicity.*

HERBERT SEYMOUR HASTINGS

The Birth of Our Lord

"And the angel said unto her,
Fear not, Mary: for thou hast found favour with **God**.
And, behold, thou shalt conceive in thy womb,
   and bring forth a son,
   and shalt call his name Jesus. . . .
And she brought forth her firstborn son,
   and wrapped him in swaddling clothes,
   and laid him in a manger."

Read Luke 2:1-7.

How strange it seems to us, as we lie in our comfortable beds, that the Lord of glory, who deserved the most luxurious cradle in all the world, should be born in a barn and cushion His downy head on a pillow of straw! How bumpy the ride must have seemed to Mary as she traveled, probably on the back of a donkey, all the way from Nazareth to Bethlehem! She may even have walked those hundred miles. Did she and Joseph understand the prophecy concerning Jesus' birthplace, or did they sometimes fear that the child might be born before they reached their destination?

The story is told of a little girl, in a well-to-do home, who said one day, "Mamma, I don't understand why, if God is so rich, He let His Son be born in a manger. Why didn't He buy Him a little bed like mine?"

We could speculate on the delivery in that unsanitary stable, the lack of an attendant physician, the simple layette which Mary had brought along from her home. But all these details are lost in the splendor of the occasion, beginning when the angel first told Mary that she was to bring forth the "Son of the Highest." The simplicity of the setting accentuates the beauty of the Child, the wonder of His coming, and the quiet worship of the first visitors who knelt at His feet. May we at this joyous time of our lives meditate on the birth of our Saviour, opening our hearts to Him as never before!

Father in heaven, who didst send Thine only Son to us as a little babe, I thank Thee for the miracle of birth. I thank Thee, too, that because a Saviour was born into this world, I can be "born again" into the kingdom of God. May the birth of my child remind me of Thy Son who came that I, believing on Him, might have life everlasting. Amen.

· 19 ·

MATERNITY

Within the crib that stands beside my bed
A little form in sweet abandon lies
And as I bend above with misty eyes
I know how Mary's heart was comforted.

O world of Mothers! blest are we who know
The ecstasy—the deep God-given thrill
That Mary felt when all the earth was still
In that Judean starlight long ago!

ANNE P. L. FIELD

Mary's Song

"And Mary said,
   My soul doth magnify the Lord,
   And my spirit hath rejoiced in God my Saviour.
   For he hath regarded the low estate of his handmaiden:
   For, behold, from henceforth all generations shall call me blessed."

Read Luke 1:46-55.

When expectant mothers get together, there is always a great deal of hopeful, animated conversation. But the famous meeting of Mary, the mother of Jesus, and Elisabeth, the mother of John the Baptist, had more than the usual amount of excitement and joy. Filled with the Holy Spirit, Elisabeth shouted,

   "Blessed are you among women,
   And blessed is your child! . . .
   For as soon as your greeting reached my ears,
   The baby leaped for joy within me!"   *(Williams Translation)*

Mary's Magnificat of thanksgiving is much like the song of Hannah. Mary, too, makes the occasion one of praise to God for His greatness, His holiness, His mercy, His strength, and His justice. In her humility she wonders at the Almighty's choice of a lowly handmaiden such as herself to be forever blessed among women.

If Mary's heart were so filled with praise before the Lord Jesus was born, can you imagine her joy when at last God Incarnate lay in her arms as a tiny babe? After the shepherds had returned to their fields, Luke tells us that "Mary kept all these things, and pondered them in her heart." Hers must have been a quiet, devout personality, for she discreetly meditated upon the momentous events of her days, looking to God for strength to face her new responsibilities.

Our task is second only to Mary's, and the God of our strength is the same loving Father who watched over the divine infant two thousand years ago. Let us, like Mary, face the future with praise, confidence, and unconquerable faith in our God.

My Father and my God, my heart has thrilled over the praise and thanksgiving of Mary, Jesus' mother. I cannot find words to express my joy as she did, but Thou knowest what is in my heart. I give Thee my wordless thanks and ask of Thee courage for the days and nights ahead. Amen.

COMETH THE CHILD

Fresh from the hand of the Father
  New from His latest creating
Clean from Love's all-golden weather
  To a bleak climate of hating
To the old failures of ages
  To a worn book, a stale story
Onto Earth's intricate pages
  Cometh the child in his glory.

Through him our purpose, once restive
  Focuses full upon duty;
Through him our joy gains refining,
  We through his eyes see new beauty.
Through him our haughty hearts crumble,
  The hills and the vales are made even;
Through him our proud souls made simple
  Find grace at the threshold of heaven.

MIRIAM SIEBER LIND

Elisabeth's Preparation

"And they were both righteous before God,
Walking in all the commandments and ordinances of
the Lord blameless."

Read Luke 1:5-17.

God, who "seeth not as man seeth . . . but . . . looketh on the heart," did not choose men and women of great worldly influence to take part in the events surrounding the birth of our Saviour. Instead He selected poor, humble, ordinary folks, people who were "walking in all the commandments and ordinances of the Lord blameless." And what better qualification for parenthood can we find than a pious, God-fearing heart such as God saw in Zacharias and Elisabeth?

Most of the account of the birth of John the Baptist describes the experiences of Zacharias, his initial sin of doubt and his final triumph of faith. But of Elisabeth we read only of her joy that the Lord had finally taken away her reproach and had answered her prayer. We see her faith, her humility, and her obedience in the naming and training of her son. What a commentary on her character, that the angel Gabriel could send the youthful Mary to Elisabeth to be strengthened in courage and in faith!

Because of her faithfulness to God, Elisabeth was able to carry out the plan which the heavenly Father had for her, and her son "continued to grow and to gain strength in the Spirit" (Luke 1:80, Williams translation).

Although the purpose of the little life at our side has not been announced to us by angels, God just as surely has a plan for him as He did for John the Baptist. Thus our song of thanksgiving should be accompanied by a prayer for inward purity, that we, too, may be prepared to carry out God's will in the training of our child.

I see, dear God, that the most important preparation for me in my duties as a mother is to live a righteous, blameless life as an example to my child. Since I cannot do this in my own strength, come into my heart and abide there. Strengthen my inner self with the presence of Thy Spirit. In Jesus' name I ask this. Amen.

· 23 ·

They say that man is mighty,
  He governs land and sea,
He wields a mighty scepter
  O'er lesser powers than he;

But mightier power and stronger
  Man from his throne has hurled,
For the hand that rocks the cradle
  Is the hand that rules the world.

W. R. WALLACE

An ounce of mother is worth a pound of clergy.

SPANISH PROVERB

Jochebed's Privilege

"And the woman conceived, and bare a son: and when she saw him that he was a goodly child, she hid him three months. And when she could not longer hide him, she took for him an ark . . . and put the child therein; and she laid it in the flags by the river's brink."

Read Exodus 2:1-10.

Little Moses was born in troublesome times, in an age when Hebrew mothers could rightly feel insecure about the future of their infant sons. So intent was Pharaoh on subduing the Jewish people, that he used every horrible method in his power to halt the increase of this minority group in his land.

We do not know much about Jochebed, Moses' mother, but we can see that she must have been endowed with a generous portion of motherly wisdom and guided by a higher power. For she actually carried out a plan which not only saved the life of her baby, but established him in the palace of the monarch who sought to destroy him.

When Moses was born, his mother was probably too busy keeping him hidden from the authorities to write a song of thanksgiving such as Hannah and Elisabeth did. But when he was three months old how she must have rejoiced! God, in His providence, had given her the privilege of caring for her son and training him in ways of righteousness for a lifetime of service. Although Jochebed did not know it then, her little son was one day to become a leader of God's people, forever remembered for his faith and obedience to God.

Certainly God is honored by our words of praise and thanksgiving, but He wants something more of us. He wants us to show our gratitude to Him by bringing up sons and daughters who, like Moses, "refuse to be called the son of Pharaoh's daughter; choosing rather to suffer affliction with the people of God, than to enjoy the pleasures of sin for a season" (Hebrews 11:24, 25).

Gracious Father, I thank Thee for the example of Jochebed, one of the great mothers of all time. If Thou couldst deliver her from such a great danger, certainly Thou canst guide me in the perplexing problems of caring for my baby. For I, too, want to take good care of my child and train him for Thy service. Amen.

· 25 ·

THE NEW BABY

"How funny and red!"
  That's what they said.
"Why, there's nothing but fuzz
  On top of his head."
And they lifted the covers
  To look at his feet.
"Oh, how tiny and wrinkled
  And red as a beet!"
And I heard them whispering
  Behind my back,
"Did you ever think
  He would look like that,
All wrinkled and red
  Like a baby bird?"
Of course they didn't
  Know that I heard.
But I had to smile
  When the baby was fed
To see how fast
  They lined up by his bed,
And in spite of the fact
  He was wrinkled and thin,
They all begged for a turn
  At holding him.

OSIE HERTZLER ZIEGLER

· 26 ·

Family Joy

"God setteth the solitary in families. . . ."

PSALM 68:6

"Thy wife shall be as a fruitful vine
  by the sides of thine house:
  thy children like olive plants
  round about thy table."

PSALM 128:3

In a day when family life is disintegrating, when selfishness breaks up homes and brings unwanted children into the world, how refreshing and how stabilizing is our never-changing God and His divine institution, the Christian home!

According to Psalm 128, it is the man that "feareth the Lord; that walketh in his ways," who finds in his wife and children the deepest and finest satisfaction. Psalm 127 says, "Happy is the man that hath his quiver full of them [children]." Of course, this "quiverful" joy of which the psalmist speaks is not selfish parental pride, which takes personal glory for a God-given gift. While "quiverful" joy does not express itself in boasting about one's children, it does bring with it, however, a wholesome type of self-respect. For the psalmist says, "They shall not be ashamed, but they shall speak with the enemies in the gate."

The woman who obeys God's call to motherhood is acting in accordance with the plan of an all-knowing God for her life. The psalmist pictures her here as a beautiful, fruitful vine, and the writer of the Proverbs says that her value is far above rubies. In motherhood, as in all areas of life, living in the will of God brings inner peace, delightful experiences, and lasting satisfaction in addition to the daily round of problems, trials, and lessons, hard-learned.

Dear Father of fathers and mothers, I thank Thee for establishing the home as a place where we can share life's most beautiful relation- *I thank Thee for making me a woman, a wife, and a mother. worthy of this call; may I make my home a joyous place. In e. Amen.*

· 27 ·

A tired old doctor died today, and a baby boy was born—
A little new soul that was pink and frail,
* and a soul that was gray and worn.*
And—halfway here and halfway there
On a white, high hill of shining air—
They met and passed and paused to speak
* in the flushed and hearty dawn.*

The man looked down at the soft, small thing,
* with wise and weary eyes;*
And the little chap stared back at him,
* with startled, scared surmise,*
And then he shook his downy head—
"I think I won't be born," he said;
"You are too gray and sad!" And he shrank
* from the pathway down the skies.*

But the tired old doctor roused once more
* at the battle-cry of birth,*
And there was memory in his look, of grief
* and toil and mirth.*
"Go on!" he said. "It's good—and bad:
It's hard! Go on! It's ours, my lad."
And he stood and urged him out of sight,
* down to the waiting earth.*

HAROLD FRANCIS BRANCH

An Even Greater Joy

"A woman when she is in travail hath sorrow, because her hour is come: but as soon as she is delivered of the child, she remembereth no more the anguish, for joy that a man is born into the world. And ye now therefore have sorrow: but I will see you again, and your heart shall rejoice, and your joy no man taketh from you."

JOHN 16:21, 22

These comforting words, which break forth with fresh meaning to the mother of a newborn baby, were spoken by our Lord to His bewildered disciples just before He left them to be with His Father. With this vivid illustration Jesus showed how the difficulties of true Christian discipleship will one day be swallowed up in everlasting happiness.

They sat dejected around their Master, those eleven disciples, wishing that He would tell of their union with Him, instead of talking about leaving for some faraway place. If only He would speak to them more plainly! They could not understand what He meant by, "A little while, and ye behold me no more; and again a little while, and ye shall see me." The strange mixture of sorrow and joy, of suffering and comfort, of trouble and peace, puzzled them deeply.

Not until after Jesus rose from His grave, went up into heaven, and poured out His Holy Spirit did the disciples fully understand, "In the world ye shall have tribulation: but be of good cheer; I have overcome the world." The Comforter *did* come and Jesus' prayer for His followers was answered with spiritual power that continued bearing fruit through the centuries.

Bringing the lesson back to us, we have already forgotten those anxious hours of labor before our baby came, in the tremendous satisfaction that he is here. How much more quickly we will forget life's problems when eternity suddenly ushers us into the long-awaited presence of our Lord Jesus Christ!

O Christ, we thank Thee for explaining the great truths of the kingdom in words we can all understand. We thank Thee for earthly joys that remind us of the pleasures of eternity with Thee. May I, today, sit in heavenly places in Thee, that in ages to come I may enjoy the exceeding riches of Thy grace in heaven itself. In Thy name I pray. Amen.

A TRIBUTE TO CHILDHOOD

When God made the child He began early in the morning. He watched the golden hues of the rising day chasing away the darkness, and He chose the azure of the opening heavens for the color of childhood's eyes, the crimson of the clouds to paint its cheeks, and the gold of the morning for its flowing tresses. He listened to the song of the birds as they sang and warbled and whispered, and strung childhood's harp with notes now soft and low—now sweet and strong.

He saw little lambs among the flock romp and play and skip, and He put play into childhood's heart. He saw the silvery brook and listened to its music and He made the laughter of the child like the ripple of the brook. He saw angels of light as upon the wings of love they hastened to holy duty, and He formed the child's heart in purity and love.

And having made the child, He sent it out to bring joy into the home, laughter on the green and gladness everywhere. He sent it into the home and said to the parents, "Nourish and bring up this child for me." He sent it to the church and said, "Teach it my love and my laws." He sent it to the state and said, "Deal tenderly with it and it will bless and not curse you." He sent it to the nation and said, "Be good to the child. It is thy greatest asset and thy hope."

GEORGE W. RIDEOUT

The Perfect Gift

"Every good and every perfect gift is from above, and cometh down from the Father of lights, with whom is no variableness, neither shadow of turning."

JAMES 1:17

A friend of ours, charmed by the joys of first parenthood, wrote us in a letter, "I still wonder at what age parents may begin to take credit for such good behavior; so far the goodness of the gift reflects the greater goodness of the Giver." We all agree that there is no age when *we* can take credit for the miracle of love which is now ours, for the gift is absolutely unmerited and the glory belongs to the King of glory!

Our wiggly little bundle came at Christmas time, reminding us in a special way that babies are remarkable gifts. Certainly no gift had ever brought with it such demands upon our time, energy, and pocketbook. But neither had any previous Christmas present brought eternal significance. A divinely planned blend of both our personalities, he was at the same time a new and living soul. Scarcely aware of anything beyond himself and his needs, he came to us with an amazing capacity for love, a love which developed and matured as he was loved by other people and learned about the love of God. And most significant of all, this gift was created by God Himself, in His own image and for His own glory. Ours for today, he is God's for eternity.

"What shall I render unto the Lord
for all his benefits toward me?
I will take the cup of salvation,
and call upon the name of the Lord.
I will pay my vows unto the Lord now
in the presence of all his people."

THE PSALMIST (PSALM 116:12-14)

· 31 ·

THE MOTHER'S HYMN

Lord who ordainest for mankind
  Benignant toils and tender cares,
We thank Thee for the ties that bind
  The mother to the child she bears.

We thank Thee for the hopes that rise
  Within her heart, as, day by day,
The dawning soul, from those young eyes,
  Looks with a clearer, steadier ray.

And grateful for the blessing given
  With that dear infant on her knee,
She trains the eye to look to heaven,
  The voice to lisp a prayer to Thee.

Such thanks the blessed Mary gave
  When from her lap the Holy Child,
Sent from on high to seek and save
  The lost of earth, looked up and smiled.

All-Gracious! grant to those who bear
  A mother's charge, the strength and light
To guide the feet that own their care
  In ways of Love and Truth and Right.

WILLIAM CULLEN BRYANT

A Psalm of Thanksgiving

"Make a joyful noise unto the Lord, all ye lands.
Serve the Lord with gladness:
Come before his presence with singing.
Know ye that the Lord he is God:
It is he that hath made us, and not we ourselves;
We are his people, and the sheep of his pasture.

"Enter into his gates with thanksgiving,
And into his courts with praise:
Be thankful unto him, and bless his name.
For the Lord is good; his mercy is everlasting;
And his truth endureth to all generations."

THE PSALMIST (PSALM 100)

II. "The Lord hath given me my petition . . ."

MEDITATIONS ON THE CHILD

TO A CHILD I KNOW

Dear little child with eyes
  Like violets glowing,
And face all dimpled with
  Enchanting smile,
You have a beauty which is
  Innocently flowing
Unhindered yet by any
  Thought of guile.
Your soul is breathing
  Peaceful as a flower,
And loving me keeps me
  In touch with love,
Before the world steps in
  I prize each precious hour,
That lifts my soul through you
  To God above.

J. M. BALLANTYNE

As a Little Child

"A little child shall lead them."

ISAIAH 11:6b

"Out of the mouth of babes and sucklings thou hast perfected praise."   MATTHEW 21:16

"And he took a child, and set him in the midst of them."

MARK 9:36

To Jesus' most intimate earthly friends, the twelve disciples, some of His words and actions were surely hard to understand. Although He was the greatest man who ever lived, the Son of the Highest, He told them that He had not come to save His life but to lose it. He came as a servant, not to be ministered unto, but to minister.

Not long after Jesus said, "If any man will come after me, let him deny himself," these poor, human disciples got into a foolish argument.

"I think *I* will be the greatest in the kingdom of heaven," was in essence what each one declared, giving no doubt his own convincing reasons.

How discouraging to the Lord Jesus, who had been trying to help them see what the *real* kingdom of God was like! But He did not rebuke them harshly. "If anyone wants to be the first, he must be the last of all and the servant of all" (Mark 9:35, Williams translation).

Then He gave them an object lesson they were not soon to forget. Drawing a little child to His bosom, He told them that if they were to enter the kingdom *at all,* they would have to become as little children. And if they were to become truly great, they must be willing to treat even little children as they would treat Him, their Lord.

It is easy to criticize those early followers, but how often we, too, are *childish* rather than *childlike.* How grateful we can be that God has set a little child in *our* midst, a little example of the simple virtues of innocence, meekness, trust, forgiveness, and love.

O Lord, Thou hast searched me and known me. Thou knowest that many times I am not childlike in spirit, but childish and selfish. Teach me, by observing my own small baby, some of the spiritual qualities Thou wouldst have me possess. Amen.

"Suffer that little children come to Me,
Forbid them not." Emboldened by His words,
The mothers onward press; but, finding vain
The attempt to reach the Lord, they trust their babe
To strangers' hands; the innocents, alarmed
Amid the throng of faces all unknown,
Shrink, trembling, till their wandering eyes discern
The countenance of Jesus, beaming love
And pity; eager then they stretch their arms,
And, cowering, lay their heads upon His breast.

JAMES GRAHAME

The Child and the Christ

"Suffer the little children to come unto me, and forbid them not: for of such is the kingdom of God. . . . Whosoever shall not receive the kingdom of God as a little child, he shall not enter therein. And he took them up in his arms, put his hands upon them, and blessed them."

MARK 10:14, 15, 16

Even though Jesus had told the disciples how valuable little children were to Him, how every child's angel has access to the Father's throne, yet Christ's first kindergarten class was almost sent away from Him by those well-meaning friends of His. Jesus said, "Stop sending them away. The kingdom belongs to little children."

Wouldn't we have enjoyed crowding near Him with our babies, hearing His soft voice call them by name, watching Him caress them? What Jesus ___ to the children we do not know, but we can be sure He neith___ ___ vn to them nor did He speak above their heads. I like ___ miling with the children; He did not tease them nor ___ me people are inclined to do. Taking them up in ___ loved them, laying the same kind hand on their ___ ht strength and healing to so many.

___ eager to bring their children to Jesus. But how ___ rts crave His fellowship? It has been said that ___ more easily to Christian teaching than older ___ are combination of curiosity and confidence, ___ nd their willingness to believe. Are we as ___ the feet of Jesus, drinking in His life-giving ___ en? We can keep on learning about God and ___ while we teach our children; while we watch Him bless ___ babies, we, too, can worship at His feet, and be blessed.

Just as the mothers long ago, dear Christ, didst bring their little ones to Thee for Thy blessing, so I bring my baby to Thee today. Take him up in Thy everlasting arms and love him, I pray. And help me always to come to Thee for blessing and inspiration. In Thy name I ask these special favors. Amen.

HE TEACHES YOU

He's greater far, that little child, than you;
The very child you teach, he teaches you.
You teach him to be Christlike, but have you
Forgotten he already is, far more than you?
You teach him right from wrong, and yet it's he,
Not you, whose conscience is more clear and free.
You teach him trust in God, but can't you see
That it is you who lack trust more than he?
For you find doubt and reason in your way
While he in simple faith believes straightway.
You teach him to forgive, but don't you know
That he forgives in half the time you do?
And he, when he forgives, at once forgets;
But you? You struggle long with grudge and debts.
You try to teach him love. You can't. You cry,
"My child, you are the teacher, and not I!"
So learn from him, be like him, you who teach.
You must, Christ says, if heaven you would reach.

IDA BOYER BONTRAGER

The Child Teaches Us Humility

"Whosoever therefore shall humble himself as this little child, the same is greatest in the kingdom of heaven."

MATTHEW 18:4

If thou, O daughter of the King, wouldst be truly humble, consider the baby which the Lord hath bestowed upon thee!

Paul once said to Timothy, "For we brought nothing into this world, and it is certain we can carry nothing out." If ever anyone came to your house with an empty suitcase, your baby did. Aside from those physical and mental capacities waiting to be developed as part of his personality, your baby came to this world empty-handed.

He came without ambition or reputation. Indeed, he can afford to be himself at all times; he never puts on a front. That word "innocence" describes how completely without worldly wisdom your little one is.

Your baby entered this world without a resentment of any kind, and it will be a long time before he learns to hold a grudge or carry ill will around on his little shoulders. May he never learn! He is a twig unbent, totally bereft of any prejudices. Humble, sincere learner that he is, he is completely teachable.

The baby enters this universe without anxiety. If he has any "fears" at all, they are not the foolish, complicated variety that haunt our grown-up lives. The baby does not trouble himself about where his next meal will come from nor what will happen to him tomorrow.

Probably the outstanding lesson Jesus wanted us to learn from the child is the lesson of *humility,* fundamental to all the other Christian graces.

To humble ourselves as a little child, we must lay aside ambition and reputation, resentments and prejudices, anxieties and materialistic concerns of this life. Stripped of the veneer of sophistication which hides our genuine selves, we must let the honest, sincere, trustful, loving, forgiving, learning child live within us.

For, "Whosoever shall not receive the kingdom of God as a little child shall in no wise enter therein."

I thank thee, O Father, Lord of heaven and earth, because thou hast hid these things from the wise and prudent, and hast revealed them unto babes (A prayer of Jesus, as recorded in Matthew 11:25).

· 41 ·

TRUST IN GOD

The child leans on its parent's breast,
Leaves there its cares and is at rest;
The bird sits singing by his nest,
  And tells aloud
His trust in God, and so is blest
  'Neath every cloud.

He has no store, he sows no seed;
Yet sings aloud, and doth not heed;
By flowing stream or grassy mead,
  He sings to shame
Men, who forget, in fear of need,
  A Father's name.

The heart that trusts for ever sings,
And feels as light as it had wings;
A well of peace within it springs;
  Come good or ill.
Whate'er today, tomorrow, brings,
  It is His will.

ISAAC WILLIAMS

The Child Teaches Us Trust

"If ye then, being evil, know how to give good gifts unto your children, how much more shall your Father which is in heaven give good things to them that ask him?"
Read Matthew 7:7-11.

When my baby was born and I saw how completely helpless and dependent he was upon me, I was frightened, for I knew my own limitations and lack of experience. It was fortunate that the baby was ignorant of his mother's woeful inexperience: otherwise he never could have slept so sweetly in his little basket!

The utter dependence of a new baby upon his mother has often been used to illustrate the helpless state in which we find ourselves, as children of our Father in heaven. Just as a mother watches over her child with unfailing love, regardless of his inability to express his needs in words and sentences, so the loving father-heart of God is sensitive to our every cry. Our Father knows what things we have need of even before we ask Him. Jesus told us that Himself.

As a child grows older, his trust in his parents becomes a more intelligent response. He sees them as people who express their love for him in many little ways. Despite a painful trip to the dentist, a dose of foul-tasting medicine, or an occasional spanking, the child knows his parents love him.

Sometimes we as Christians are faced with situations which try us and for which we, like Job, can see no reason.

Our trust in God, to be really perfect and childlike, must accept the higher wisdom of His love in difficult situations as well as when things are going our way. Paul's advice to the Philippians on prayerful trust is "good for what ails us" today. Let's put it to practice!

"Be careful for nothing; but in every thing by prayer and supplication with thanksgiving let your requests be made known unto God.

"And the peace of God, which passeth all understanding, shall keep your hearts and minds through Christ Jesus."

PHILIPPIANS 4:6, 7

My loving Father in heaven, how glad I am that I can relax in the thought of Thy tender concern for me. Just as my baby trusts in me completely, so I rest in the security of Thy love. Give me the inner peace that manifests itself in strength and poise. In the name of Thy Son I ask this. Amen.

SAVIOUR, TEACH ME DAY BY DAY

Saviour, teach me day by day
Love's sweet lesson to obey;
Sweeter lesson cannot be:
Loving Him who first loved me.

With a childlike heart of love,
At Thy bidding may I move,
Prompt to serve and follow Thee—
Loving Him who first loved me.

JANE E. LEESON

The Child Teaches Us the Love of the Father

"As one whom his mother comforteth, so will I comfort you."   ISAIAH 66:13a

"Like as a father pitieth his children, so the Lord pitieth them that fear him."   PSALM 103:13

A young mother, noticing that the baby of the family was not benefiting from her Bible story hour with the older children, decided that she would show him the love of the heavenly Father in a way he could better understand—by taking him in her arms and rocking him. As she sat thus meditating and cuddling him, her own spiritual life was enriched and strengthened.

A dear old disciple of Christ, eighty-nine years of age, once said that although he was the fifteenth child in his family, he always believed that his mother loved him best of all. During the many years that followed his babyhood, the memory of that loving Christian mother pointed him to a heavenly Father who comforts like a mother and pities as an earthly father.

As much as we love our babies, we know that God the Father loves us with a more perfect love. We are such imperfect symbols of God's parental affection, for our Father is never annoyed when we cry. He is never physically tired. He never slumbers nor sleeps. He watches over us with even deeper concern than we have for our own little sleepers. How warm, how secure, how comforting it is to have a God like that!

One evening, as I sat feeding my baby, he suddenly stopped eating, laid his head against my shoulder, and touching my cheek with his chubby little hand, said, "Ah, Ah." As I pondered this little note of endearment, I came to the conclusion that true worship is probably nothing more than touching the kind cheek of the heavenly Father and whispering, "Ah, Ah, dear Father."

Oh, that my worship of Thee, dear God, would be as free and spontaneous as the love of a little child for his mother. Help me to nurture my babe in such a tender way that when we tell him of Thy love, he will understand and love Thee in response. Amen.

· 45 ·

FAITH OF OUR MOTHERS

Faith of our mothers, living yet
*   In cradle song and bedtime prayer,*
In nursery love and fireside lore,
*   Thy presence still pervades the air.*
Faith of our mothers, living faith,
We will be true to thee till death.

Faith of our mothers, lavish faith,
*   The fount of childhood's trust and grace,*
O may thy consecration prove
*   The wellspring of a nobler race.*
Faith of our mothers, lavish faith,
We will be true to thee till death.

Faith of our mothers, guiding faith,
*   For youthful longings—youthful doubts,*
How blurred our vision, blind our way,
*   Thy providential care without.*
Faith of our mothers, guiding faith,
We will be true to thee till death.

Faith of our mothers, Christian faith,
*   In truth beyond our man-made creeds,*
Still serve the home and save the church,
*   And breathe thy spirit through our deeds.*
Faith of our mothers, Christian faith,
We will be true to thee till death.

ARTHUR B. PATTEN

The Child Our Imitator

"When I call to remembrance the unfeigned faith that is in thee, which dwelt first in thy grandmother Lois, and thy mother Eunice; and I am persuaded that in thee also."

II TIMOTHY 1:5

"When I grow up I want to be just like Mother (or Daddy)," is a more sobering statement than we perhaps think. For children are little imitators, every one of them, and they are going to imitate and grow to be like those with whom they live. The story is told of a little girl who was heard screeching at her dolls. When her mother asked the reason, she replied that she was playing "Mamma."

There are many vital habits which the child picks up unconsciously from his parents—little mannerisms, polite or rude manners, a sunny or a grouchy disposition, neat or slovenly appearance, good or bad attitudes, words, and actions.

Seeing his own faults and virtues "on parade" in his children has a rather startling effect on the average parent. Joseph Joubert, in the year 1842, expressed a great truth when he said, "Children need models more than they need critics." Children are quick to notice if we preach one thing and practice another in our everyday life. Nor can we hide unkind attitudes or other inconsistencies, thinking that our children will not see our real selves.

The Apostle Paul told his followers, "Be ye followers of me, even as I also am of Christ." Can we sincerely ask our little ones to follow us as *we* follow Christ? Are we passing on to them our strong faith, manifested in our every word and action?

> I tried to lead a child through play
> To grow more Christlike every day
> And I myself became that way.
> MABEL NIEDERMEYER McCAW

Dear Christ, this tiny baby, now so unconscious of all that is going on about him, will soon be watching and imitating the things I do. May I so closely imitate Thee that I will not need to fear my influence on his young life. Conform me, O Christ, to Thine own image, that my children may see the beauty of Jesus in me. Amen.

I WOULD BE TRUE

I would be true, for there are those who trust me;
  I would be pure, for there are those who care;
I would be strong, for there is much to suffer;
  I would be brave, for there is much to dare.

I would be friend of all—the foe, the friendless;
  I would be giving, and forget the gift;
I would be humble, for I know my weakness;
  I would look up, and live, and love, and lift.

HOWARD ARNOLD WALTER

The Child Our Challenge to Pure Living

"Create in me a clean heart, O God; and renew a
right spirit within me."   PSALM 51:10

Have you ever cuddled your baby to your breast and said to him,
perhaps not aloud, "You dear, innocent little soul, what a wretched
old world I've brought you into"? I have. But I've gotten over wor-
rying about what will become of him in the far-flung years of the
future. For the most formative period of his life are those years with
me before he ever faces that dubious, unreliable character, John Q.
Public.

While my little fellow is still tagging on to the hem of my gar-
ment, he is going to be getting his basic training in life. As we noticed
yesterday, he's going to imitate me, to gradually imbibe my actions
and reactions, my habits and attitudes. This calls for scrupulous self-
examination on my part and daily cleansing at the cross of Christ.
What a challenge to pure living is the unstained life of a little child!

But how do we fit the devotional life into our busy mother sched-
ules? When we are consciously walking with God, we are surprised
at our many opportunities for informal fellowship with Him. Those
pleasant periods when nursing or rocking our babies can well be used
for meditation on a spiritual truth we need at the moment, for give-
and-take conversation with the Lord, for thanksgiving and praise. We
can memorize hymns as we iron; we can paste a precious Scripture
above the kitchen sink. We can bring such big-little things to God
as the formula we are mixing or the baby's colic.

The unblemished life of a newborn babe does indeed have a
purifying influence on the lives of Christian parents. And it is only by
keeping our own hearts and minds centered on the Lord Jesus Christ,
that we will be able to lead our children into "whatsoever things are
true . . . honest . . . just . . . pure . . . lovely . . . of good report."

*Dear Jesus, I thank Thee that Thou art interested in every detail
of my life. Help me to worship Thee as I go about my daily routine.
Give me the grace to live above petty irritations and fretful worries.
And when I fail, create in me a clean heart, O God, and renew a right
spirit within me. Amen.*

· 49 ·

TIME-HONORED TRUTH

The statement may seem very trite,
  It has been said so often,
That babies have been sent from heav'n
  Our calloused hearts to soften.

But though the story may be old,
  It's changed no jot or tittle,
The baby is God's messenger
  E'en though he is so little.

And so I feel the aged truth
  Needs no fresh interpretation—
A baby's face is heaven's grace
  To any generation.

HELEN GOOD BRENNEMAN

The Child, Preserver of Life Values

"Hear, ye children, the instruction of a father,
   and attend to know understanding.
For I give you good doctrine, forsake ye not my law.
For I was my father's son, tender and only beloved
   in the sight of my mother.
He taught me also, and said unto me,
Let thine heart retain my words:
Keep my commandments, and live."

PROVERBS 4:1-4

In the days when the great-grandchildren of the aged Joseph were brought to his knees to be blessed, people considered it a high privilege to become acquainted with and to influence one's posterity. In Psalm 128:6 we read, "Yea, thou shalt see thy children's children, and peace upon Israel," a promise made to the man who feared the Lord. Proverbs 17:6 states, "Children's children are the crown of old men; and the glory of children are their fathers."

One day my husband and I were invited as guests to a large family reunion. The carry-in dinner was spread on long tables; the picnic grounds were dotted with cousins of every age and size. To our surprise we were informed that all these people, despite their differences in personality and appearance, were by birth or marriage direct descendants of one couple just a few generations back. We could only wonder what a family reunion several years hence would reveal in our own children and our children's children. Will our Christian nurture be strong and winsome enough to bear fruit in future generations? What ideals will we plant in our young, what values will we teach as important?

In our children we have an opportunity to live again, for the child is a preserver of our life values; thus may we strive for the highest goals in life, as did one minister who said, "If we cannot leave a single dollar to our children, let us give them the more important heritage of godly Christian parents."

Gracious God, I thank Thee for strong family ties that bind us together with those we love. I thank Thee for my own parents and grandparents who taught me principles of right living. Bless the baby's grandparents, give wisdom to us his parents, and help us all to inspire him to love and follow Thee. Amen.

· 51 ·

Not in the clamor of the crowded street,
Not in the shouts and plaudits of the throng,
But in ourselves are triumph and defeat.

HENRY WADSWORTH LONGFELLOW

"He that ruleth his spirit [is better] than he that taketh
a city." PROVERBS 16:32b

The Child an Individual

"And the Lord God formed man of the dust of the ground, and breathed into his nostrils the breath of life; and man became a living soul." GENESIS 2:7

Before we close the section of meditations on the child and his meaning to us, we must consider him in his own right, as a new and separate individual. Though he may look like Uncle John and have ears like his mother's side of the family, God has given him a personality all his own, one which like a bud will gradually unfold before our wondering eyes.

Alta Mae Erb, in her book on *The Christian Nurture of Children,* says that a child's personality is determined by: his inherited possibilities, his physical body, his surroundings, his own individual self, and salvation of this self through Christ. And strange as it may seem, the first six months of one's life are very significant, for the many influences on a child's personality begin operating powerfully when he is still a babe-in-arms.

To ignore the rights of a little child as a person is unkind and unjust. He is not a grownup in miniature form and dare not be treated as such. His personality needs to be respected, and we need to build solid character and lofty ideals upon his own particular characteristics and needs. Although we cannot preach sermons to him when he is only three weeks old, we can start developing the text of our lifetime sermon: love. For the love of two emotionally mature Christian parents is our baby's greatest need.

Delicate plants require patient, skillful, loving care. How much more does the sensitive personality of a little child need the sunshine of our love and the careful nurture of sympathizing parents. What a privilege and what a *responsibility* it is for us to guard the development of an immortal soul!

Dear God, in view of all that is expected of a mother, I would feel most inadequate were not my hand in Thine. I thank Thee for entrusting me with a living soul. Help me to bring out the best that is in him, teaching him above all things to live, move, and have his being in Thee. In Jesus' name. Amen.

· 53 ·

THE CHILD'S APPEAL

I am the Child.
All the world waits for my coming.
All the earth watches with interest to see what I shall become.
Civilization hangs in the balance,
For what I am, the world of tomorrow will be.

I am the Child.
I have come into your world, about which I know nothing.
Why I came I know not;
How I came I know not.
I am curious; I am interested.

I am the Child.
You hold in your hand my destiny.
You determine, largely, whether I shall succeed or fail.
Give me, I pray you, those things that make for happiness.
Train me, I beg you, that I may be a blessing to the world.

MAMIE GENE COLE

The Child Our Trust

"Therefore let no man glory in men. For all things are yours . . . the world . . . life . . . death . . . things present . . . things to come; all are yours; and ye are Christ's; and Christ is God's." I CORINTHIANS 3:21-23

Of all the challenging truths which we, like Mary, have pondered in our hearts since our baby's birth, our small part in creating an everlasting soul is surely the most awe-inspiring. Masefield states the majesty of giving birth to a child in the words:

"And he who gives a child a treat
Makes joy-bells ring in Heaven's street,
And he who gives a child a home
Builds palaces in Kingdom come,
And she who gives a baby birth
Brings Saviour Christ again to Earth."*

One evening my husband and I called in the home of new parents and found them sitting blissfully in their living room, watching the sleeping infant with quiet satisfaction. "Such a sweet little life God has given us to care for," the mother whispered. "Just think, he is really not ours, but God's."

I like to think of the security of a baby born in a Christian home. In a way, we can call the baby our own, but since we are Christ's and Christ is God's, the baby ultimately belongs to Him. How secure our children are in the close relationship of God's "family tree": baby, mother, father, Christ, God!

Thus, as we meditate upon our child we think of him as our *trust*, the one whom God has given us in stewardship to bring up for Him. Like the mother of Samson we cry at this point, "Teach us what we shall do unto the child. . . ." And how ready our heavenly Father is to do just that!

I gladly take, kind Father, this trust which Thou hast bestowed upon me. I thank Thee for the lovely dependence of a baby upon his parents, of one parent upon the other, and of both parents upon Thee. Therefore I do not take the responsibilities of motherhood upon my own shoulders alone. In Thee I go forward with confidence. Amen.

*John Masefield, *The Everlasting Mercy*

III. "Therefore also I have lent him to the Lord . . ."

OUR RESPONSIBILITY TO THE CHILD

FOR MATTHEW

Dear Little One,
Our newest, tenderest son,
What world we brought you to, we cannot know.

Neither did Hannah know
As on her happy heart sweet Samuel lay
A very Yes of God.

Neither did Eunice know
As, prattling prayers, the tiny Timothy stood
Within her circling arms.

Nor did the saintly Monica foresee
If her Augustine's world should thrive or split;

And that unique Susannah, tutoring
Young John, small Charles,
She knew no more than they . . .

Than I. But I do know,
As faith-filled they too knew,
That if your times be anguished or be still
It is God's will
That you should live therein to His high praise.

And so I singing hold you to myself.
In strong sweet faith I sing;
Our little son,
Dear, newest, tenderest One.

MIRIAM SIEBER LIND

Dedicating and Educating

"Therefore . . . I have lent him to the Lord."
I SAMUEL 1:28

We all admire the woman Hannah, who prayed for Samuel, thanked God for his coming, and dedicated him to Jehovah, making what seems to us a supreme sacrifice. At the same time we wonder what we have in common with her experience, for we keep our children, do we not? We do not take them to a temple and give them to an old man to take care of. That was what God asked of Hannah, but He asks us not only to *dedicate* but also to *educate* our children.

Exactly how long Hannah had her son with her we do not know, but women those days did not wean their children as early as we do now. On the basis of Jewish customs some Bible students believe that she took Samuel to the temple only for a visit during his infancy and then left him there when he was six years old. Be that as it may, after she had placed his dimpled hand in the wrinkled one of Eli, Hannah's task was done, except for her trip each year to take him the new coat she had made so carefully for him.

There probably isn't one of us who would want to trade places with Hannah. Yet, when we dedicate our babies to the Lord we, too, make a sobering commitment. He may take them home to be with Him if it is His will; if He leaves them with us we will lead them in paths of righteousness, trusting that they will sometime dedicate their *own* young lives to His service.

A look at the One to whom we dedicate, however, takes away any haunting dread of releasing to the Lord what seems to be ours. And one look at Him who "shall gather the lambs with his arm, and carry them in his bosom, and . . . gently lead those that are with young" sets us free from those foolish worries that ordinarily trouble us. It is in dedication that we, like Hannah, find a new and triumphant peace.

Since Thou, O God, didst give to us Thine only Son, in perfect love, I gladly dedicate my child to Thee. Work out Thy plan for his life; use him in Thy service. And with this dedication I surrender any anxious thoughts, conscious or subconscious, concerning his health, safety, and future. In the name of Jesus. Amen.

· 59 ·

THE HOUSEWIFE

Jesus, teach me how to be
Proud of my simplicity.

Sweep the floors, wash the clothes,
Gather for each vase a rose.

Iron and mend a tiny frock
Taking notice of the clock,

Always having time kept free
For childish questions asked of me.

Grant me wisdom Mary had
When she taught her little Lad.

CATHERINE CATE COBLENTZ

His Physical Care

"And whosoever shall give to drink unto one of these little ones a cup of cold water only in the name of a disciple, Verily I say unto you, he shall in no wise lose his reward."

MATTHEW 10:42

One of the hardest things to understand about our God is how He can on one hand rule the universe in infinite power, and at the same time keep an accurate record of the number of hairs on our head. Since our finite minds cannot grasp such a complex system of eternal bookkeeping, we of little faith find it difficult to believe that we shall be rewarded for so small a service as a cup of cold water given in the name of Jesus.

Have you ever wondered how far around the world a two-year diaper wash would go, if all the diapers you launder in that time were hung on a clothesline side by side? Have you ever been tempted to think that you had nothing to show for your day's work after a day in which the baby took more care than usual, perhaps crying a great deal and making extra laundry? If you have ever felt that all the detailed, intimate, time-consuming duties that go with the physical care of a baby are unnoticed by God, then reread Matthew 10:42.

Helping the newborn infant to satisfy his biological needs, such as sucking, sleeping, feeling the mother's gentle touch, and so on, is an important part of mothering. We are told that the way a mother feeds, washes, or diapers her baby conveys to him her love and concern even before he can understand the meaning of her words. How important, then, it is that we perform these duties in a spirit of love and devotion.

We care for our babies in the name of Christ when we do each little task as unto Him, putting love into everything we do. We do all our daily work in Christ's name when we seek His guidance and blessing, even on the smallest duties of our days.

Heavenly Father, I never realized how many problems a new mother faces until I became a mother myself. I thank Thee for the many helpful books on child care and for kind friends and good doctors who are ready to give a word of encouragement and assistance. As I follow my daily schedule of feeding, bathing, diapering, and comforting my baby, may I seek Thy help in each small task, doing it all with tender care, as unto Thee. Amen.

· 61 ·

BABY'S SMILE

The doctors and the nurses state
  My baby's smile's a fake.
It's not a smile at all, they say,
  It's just the tummy ache.

But Grandma's explanation
  Is much nicer, far, than this—
An angel stooped from heaven
  And gave my babe a kiss.

                          HELEN GOOD BRENNEMAN

His Emotional Care

"That they may teach the young women to be sober,
to love their husbands, to love their children."

TITUS 2:4

"Say, Mamma, let's laugh." With these words one little fellow told his mother that he needed some fun, a bit of her joyous companionship. Perhaps the mother was very busy at the moment and did not sense that her child felt just a little lonely, that he needed her. Is that not the trouble with us mammas? We are sometimes so busy taking care of our children's physical bodies, that we forget their inner need, their emotional care.

Those who study children tell us that pleasant experiences cause children to develop feelings of love and that "bad" children are often "unhappy" children. Insufficient parental affection is bound to show up in a child's personality and behavior, for little children just do not develop as they should, physically, mentally, or spiritually, when their hunger for love is not satisfied.

One doctor, in speaking of a child's need for love, made this statement: "The newly born infant needs to feel mother's bodily contacts, her light caresses; he needs to hear her soft words of delight, and to have prompt attention to his every physical need. At all ages he needs to feel that he is wanted and loved, not so much because of his being good but because he is himself."

Although God has bountifully blessed us with a natural love for our babies, we need to learn to express the love meaningfully to the child. Giving intelligent love takes time, thought, and patience, and like vitamins is a daily requirement. But the confidence our children have in us, and the companionship they share with us, will be well worth all the time and energy we invest in demonstrating to them how much we love them.

O God, Thou art love itself, and Thou hast shed light and love into my soul. Only Thou, dear Father, knowest how the seams of my heart are bursting with affection for this little mite. Help me to remember that life out in this world is very different from the security and warmth of my body, where he lived the first nine months of his existence. Help me to hold him tenderly; help him to understand that he is loved and wanted. Amen.

· 63 ·

THE TEACHER

Lord, who am I to teach the way
  To little children day by day,
  So prone myself to go astray?

I teach them knowledge, but I know
  How faint the flicker and how low
  The candles of my knowledge glow.

I teach them power to will and do,
  But only now to learn anew
  My own great weakness through and through.

I teach them love for all mankind
  And all God's creatures, but I find
  My love comes lagging far behind.

Lord, if their guide I still must be,
  Oh, let the little children see
  The teacher leaning hard on Thee.

LESLIE PINCKNEY HILL

His Intellectual Care

"And thou shalt teach them [God's commandments] diligently unto thy children, and shalt talk of them when thou sittest in thine house, and when thou walkest by the way, and when thou liest down, and when thou risest up."

DEUTERONOMY 6:7

Does a child really learn half of all he will ever know by the time he is three years old, as some people believe? If he does, then H. W. Beecher's statement, "The mother's heart is the child's schoolroom," is a real challenge to mothers.

What kind of intellectual care will our baby get while he is still in our "schoolroom," long before he ever actually goes to school? What courses will we teach him? Will his surrounding classroom (our home) be artistic and teach him the meaning of beauty? Will his playground equipment (his toys) teach him to do constructive things? Will we carefully answer his questions? Will there be good books and good music to develop his early tastes? Most important of all, will the Bible be the chief book in our library?

Most people think that the public school alone educates their children. This is a serious mistake. By the time those curls and pigtails bob into a schoolroom, the children should have completed many courses in Christian living: obedience, respect for parents and teachers, love for others, love for God. They should have had many other classes, too: handicraft, drawing, music, home economics, etc. Daddy as President, Mother as Dean, and both as Instructors should have been educating ever since the babies first began to co-ordinate mind and muscle in the world's greatest school—the home.

Long ago Solomon said, "For as he *thinketh* in his heart, so is he." And Jesus said, "Thou shalt love the Lord thy God with all thy heart, and with all thy soul, and with all thy strength, and with all thy *mind.*"

O Lord, I thank Thee for the privilege of playing with my baby, of surrounding him with worth-while toys and books and music, of teaching him the many basic lessons of life. May he learn, as he grows older, that Thou art the source of all beauty, all knowledge, and all wisdom. This I ask in Thy most worthy name. Amen.

· 65 ·

AT FOUR WEEKS

His tiny fists are clenched above his head—
His fair, round face is sweet in infant sleep—
And as I finger fringes of the shawl
That lies so slight and soft against my dress,
I pray for him:
   Lord, may he love this place—
   This house of Thine, erected by Thy grace
   Where Thy dear Word is taught, Thy praises sung.
   Oh, true, he is so very, very young
   And he may cry within these walls, or shout
   In happy, babyish mischief, or call out
   To Daddy in the pulpit. True, he may
   Not understand what Daddy has to say—
   The implications of the Trinity
   Or what "Atonement" means to him and me.
   It may be, first, that folding hands in prayer
   Is all the fellowship his soul can share.
   But as his Saviour grew, oh, may he grow.
   In sure and silent ways, may his heart know
   That Thou art here. And may my conduct be
   A commentary on my love to Thee—
   An explanation louder than my speech
   To reach where Daddy's sermons may not reach.
The singing is resumed; the Scripture's read . . .
The tiny fists now stir above his head.
A little dream-smile flits across his face.
Oh, may he learn to love this holy place!

MIRIAM SIEBER LIND

His Spiritual Care

"Train up a child in the way he should go: and when he is old, he will not depart from it."   PROVERBS 22:6

"Bring them up in the nurture and admonition of the Lord."   EPHESIANS 6:4b

How many times Jesus expressed His love and respect for little children! On that sacred day in Peter's life when Jesus asked him three times over if he really loved Him, He charged him first of all to feed His lambs, and then He told him to feed His sheep. Of every Christian parent Christ expects spiritual care of the little ones. "Mother, do you really love me? Then feed my lambs."

It matters *what* we feed little lambs. We do not take them out on the hillside and give them large tufts of stout wire grass. Likewise, a child understands and digests only those spiritual truths which fit into his own limited experience. We must know God's Word, know our children, and then adapt our singing and teaching to the understanding of the child.

How we feed the lambs is also important. One well-meaning father forced his hungry little boy to learn a verse of Scripture every morning before breakfast. The boy naturally grew to dislike the Bible. Unwise parents have been known to use Bible reading as punishment for their children. How could these children grow up to love the Word of God?

The *when* and *where* of lamb feeding is all time and everywhere. Robbie Trent, in *Your Child and God,* says, "Shall I teach my child of God? I am answering that question every day. For good or for ill, positively or negatively, for faith or for fear, I am teaching my child of God."

There will be times when we give our lambs direct nurture: Bible stories, verses, hymns, and prayers, Sunday-school and church experiences. But the indirect nurture of love and faithfulness in all our ways make the words meaningful when we tell the little ones of their loving heavenly Father.

Our Father, we cannot yet teach this tiny child to pray. But help us, his mother and father, to treat him and each other in such a way that when he does talk with Thee, he will know that Thou art kind and good and loving and just and forgiving. Amen.

WHERE DID HE GO?

I'll only have this little boy but once.
Sometime, a few years hence,
You'll come to visit, and you'll ask,
"Where did that little tousled-headed,
    brown-eyed infant go?"
And I will say,
"I do not really know.
I only know that now a man,
Tall, self-possessed, intelligent,
Is here instead.
But where that scamp'ring little fellow went,
The one who threw my good shoes out the door
And tossed his dinner plate upon the floor
And tore the pages from my best-loved book
And haunted every corner, crevice, nook,
I do not know, I cannot really say
Just where he went, but here to stay
Is this tall lad—
Our little boy in larger garments clad."

HELEN GOOD BRENNEMAN

Sweet childish days, that were as long
    As twenty days are now.

W. WORDSWORTH

Watching Him Grow

"And the child grew, and waxed strong in spirit, filled
with wisdom:
And the grace of God was upon him."   LUKE 2:40

A very little boy I once knew came running in to his mother one
day, laughing heartily at a joke on an older friend of the family.

"He waved at me. He thought I was Daddy."

And that is how it seemed to the little fellow, less than five years
old. To small children the world does not look the same as it does to
older people. That is why they are so often misunderstood.

Each stage of a child's life is different, and wonderful! When
children are still tiny babies, it sometimes seems that they do something new and startling every day. We need to understand the changes
they are making and their special needs at various ages, so that we can
more intelligently help them. There is nothing more thrilling than
watching them grow, but we dare not simply sit back and watch, for
we must guide them in developing their powers to the fullest. We
must direct their energies into constructive and worth-while channels.

The study of child nature will help us to understand and solve
the problems confronting us and our little ones. Reading good books
on child development is a wise investment of time and money for any
parent. Of course, since doctors and research students who study and
write about child growth are not always Christian, we must read their
books with discretion, remembering that our children can never be
really "good" without the help of God.

And what a unique privilege we have, as Christian parents, of
going to God's Word for the basic principles in solving all our problems in life! For we want our children, like the little boy Jesus, not
only to grow and to wax strong in spirit, increasing in wisdom, but to
experience the grace of God upon their lives.

*All-wise Father, we thank Thee for the changes that time brings
upon all of us: for growth of little children, for maturity that comes
with the years. We would not have our children remain babes, either
physically, emotionally, intellectually, or spiritually. As this infant
grows, day by day, into childhood and adulthood help me, his mother,
to guide his feet in the narrow path that leads to life. Amen.*

A MOTHER'S PRAYER

Father in heaven, make me wise,
  So that my gaze may never meet
A question in my children's eyes.
  God keep me always kind and sweet,

And patient, too, before their need;
  Let each vexation know its place,
Let gentleness be all my creed,
  Let laughter live upon my face!

A mother's day is very long,
  There are so many things to do!
But never let me lose my song
  Before the hardest day is through.

MARGARET E. SANGSTER

Wisdom for Today

"If any of you lack wisdom, let him ask of God, that giveth to all men liberally, and upbraideth not; and it shall be given him. But let him ask in faith, nothing wavering."
"Be not wise in your own conceits."

JAMES 1:5, 6 AND ROMANS 12:16c

Oh, for just a little of the wisdom of Solomon, we cry, looking at the responsibilities placed on our mother shoulders and then at our own weak selves! How can we lead our little ones in straight paths when we ourselves have so many unsolved problems? We can see the mistakes of others, but how can we be sure that we will not make some which are just as bad, or even worse?

But He who said that His strength is made perfect in our weakness can use our very mistakes to show us His better way. Even Solomon himself uttered this prayer: "And now, O Lord my God, thou hast made thy servant king instead of David my father: *and I am but a little child:* I know not how to go out or come in. . . . Give therefore thy servant an understanding heart. . . ."

God honored Solomon's prayer, and in Ephesians 1:17 we are told that we today may be given "the spirit of wisdom and revelation in the knowledge of him." To every believing Christian the Holy Spirit is promised, and He it is who will lead us into all truth.

"I said to the man who stood at the gate of the years,
  'Give me a light that I may find my way.'
But he replied,
  'Go out into the darkness and put your hand in
    the hand of God.
  This will be better than light
  And safer than a known way.' "

AUTHOR UNKNOWN

My loving heavenly Father, I praise Thee for the way that Thou hast guided my feet until this day, even though I often plod along in the darkness alone, forgetting Thy interest in my life. Gladly do I place my hand in Thine. Humbly do I ask Thy wisdom and Thy strength. Give therefore Thy servant an understanding heart. In Jesus' name. Amen.

· 71 ·

WHAT GOD HATH PROMISED

God hath not promised
  Skies always blue,
Flower-strewn pathways
  All our lives through;
God hath not promised
  Sun without rain,
Joy without sorrow,
  Peace without pain.

But God hath promised
  Strength for the day,
Rest for the labor,
  Light for the way,
Grace for the trials,
  Help from above,
Unfailing sympathy,
  Undying love.

ANNIE JOHNSON FLINT

Strength for Today

"I can do all things through Christ which strengtheneth me."
PHILIPPIANS 4:13

"My grace is sufficient for thee:
For my strength is made perfect in weakness."
II CORINTHIANS 12:9a

During the early months following the birth of a new baby, we mothers feel like a friend of mine who crossed the Atlantic in a four-motor plane which was only operating on two motors because of engine trouble. Just as her trip, instead of being quick and pleasant, was long and tedious, so the routine work which we usually enjoy becomes somewhat laborious.

But it is important that we accept this fact as a very small inconvenience for so great a gift, that we remember it is only a temporary experience and common to womankind, and that we do not let our spiritual vim and vigor lag with our physical.

For it is of spiritual strength that the Prophet Isaiah writes:
"He giveth power to the faint; and to them that have no might
    he increaseth strength. . . .
But they that wait upon the Lord shall renew their strength;
    they shall mount up with wings as eagles;
    they shall run, and not be weary;
    and they shall walk, and not faint."

Let us not, however, waste our energies and our strength and then expect God to renew them. If we are to regain our old vitality, we must observe the laws of health: get plenty of rest, the right kind of food, sufficient vitamins. We can serve simple meals, sit down to do some routine chores, lie down with our babies when we nurse them.

God promises strength, as well as material blessings, in one-day doses only. If we wait upon Him and use common sense in the use of our limited energies, we can be assured that He will give "strength for today and bright hope for tomorrow."

O God, I thank Thee for the power which Thou givest to the faint. I know that it will not be long until I once more can run and not be weary, and walk and not faint. Until then, O Father, teach me to be patient. Give me the grace and wisdom to conserve my energies for the most important tasks. In Jesus' name I ask this. Amen.

THE LORD IS MY SHEPHERD

"The Lord is my shepherd;
I shall not want.

He maketh me to lie down in green pastures:
He leadeth me beside the still waters.
He restoreth my soul:
He leadeth me in the paths of righteousness
for his name's sake.

Yea, though I walk through the valley of the shadow of death,
I will fear no evil:
For thou art with me;
Thy rod and thy staff they comfort me.

Thou preparest a table before me
In the presence of mine enemies:
Thou anointest my head with oil;
My cup runneth over.

Surely goodness and mercy shall follow me all the days of my life:
And I will dwell in the house of the Lord for ever."

PSALM 23

Courage for Today

"Be strong and of a good courage;
　Be not afraid, neither be thou dismayed:
　For the Lord thy God is with thee whithersoever thou goest."

JOSHUA 1:9

Our Task:
　"Bring them up in the nurture and admonition of the Lord."

EPHESIANS 6:4b

Our Goal:
"And this is life eternal, that they might know thee the only true God, and Jesus Christ whom thou hast sent."　　　JOHN 17:3

Our Resources:
　"Wherefore take unto you the whole armour of God . . .
　　having your loins girt about with truth,
　　and having on the breastplate of righteousness;
　　and your feet shod with the preparation of the gospel of peace:
　Above all, taking the shield of faith . . .
　　and take the helmet of salvation,
　　and the sword of the Spirit, which is the word of God."

EPHESIANS 6:13-17

Our God:
　". . . and, lo, I am with you alway, even unto the end of the world."

MATTHEW 28:20b

Prayer for Today: Repeat thoughtfully Psalm 23.

Lord, Make Me a Channel of Thy Peace,

That where there is hatred I may bring love,
That where there is wrong I may bring the spirit of forgiveness,
That where there is discord I may bring harmony,
That where there is error I may bring truth,
That where there is doubt I may bring faith,
That where there is despair I may bring hope,
That where there are shadows I may bring light,
That where there is sadness I may bring joy.

Lord, Grant That I May Seek Rather

To comfort than to be comforted,
To understand than to be understood,
To love than to be loved;
                    for
It is by giving that one receives,
It is by self-forgetting that one finds,
It is by dying that one awakens to eternal life.

ST. FRANCIS OF ASSISI

The Rewards of Motherhood

"Who can find a virtuous woman?
For her price is far above rubies."

PROVERBS 31:10

After reading King Solomon's account of the ceaseless activity of the virtuous woman, who "riseth . . . while it is yet night," and of her never-tiring efforts to look well to the ways of her household, someone who does not understand mothers might be tempted to ask what *she* gets out of it all.

Motherhood, however, does not need to seek rewards. There are ample compensations and many daily "surprise packages." As St. Francis prayed, "It is by giving that one receives . . . by self-forgetting that one finds." Solomon describes in detail many of the duties of the Christian wife and mother, but a careful reading shows that she is not a slave to be pitied. Here are a few of her rewards:

The heart of her husband doth safely trust in her.

She is not afraid of the snow for her household.

Her husband is known in the gates.

Her children . . . call her blessed.

Her husband . . . praiseth her.

She shall rejoice in time to come.

Of course, we do not work for praise; indeed, if we look for it we shall not find it. Love seeketh not her own. Nor do we care for flattery.

Like other human beings, mother needs occasionally to be reassured that she is making her loved ones happy. But her children pay her the highest tribute when they love and serve Him who once said of a woman, "She hath done what she could."

Prayer for Today: Read the prayer of St. Francis of Assisi on opposite page.

Acknowledgments

The publisher attempted to trace the ownership of all poems and quotations and to the best of his knowledge has secured all necessary permissions from authors or holders of copyrights. Should there be any oversight in making proper acknowledgment, upon notification of the same the publisher will be pleased to correct such omissions in any future editions of this publication.

For permission to reprint from copyrighted works, the author and publisher are indebted to the sources listed below.

W. W. Coblentz for the poem "The Housewife" by Catherine Cate Coblentz from *Christ and the Fine Arts*, Harper and Brothers (1938).

Macmillan Company for the poem "Everlasting Mercy" from *Poems* by John Masefield, The Macmillan Company.

Cynthia Pearl Maus for the poem "A Mother" Author Unknown from *Christ and the Fine Arts*, Harper and Brothers (1938).

Mabel Niedermeyer McCaw for the poem "I Tried to Lead a Child Through Play."

Moody Press for the passages quoted from *The New Testament*, Tr. Charles B. Williams, Moody Press (1937).

Robbie Trent for a quotation from *Your Child and God* by Robbie Trent, Harper and Brothers (1952).

Charles L. Wallis for the poem "A Mother's Prayer" by Margaret E. Sangster from *Masterpieces of Religious Verse*, Harper and Brothers (1948).